# 101

## ESSENTIAL TIPS

# TENNIS

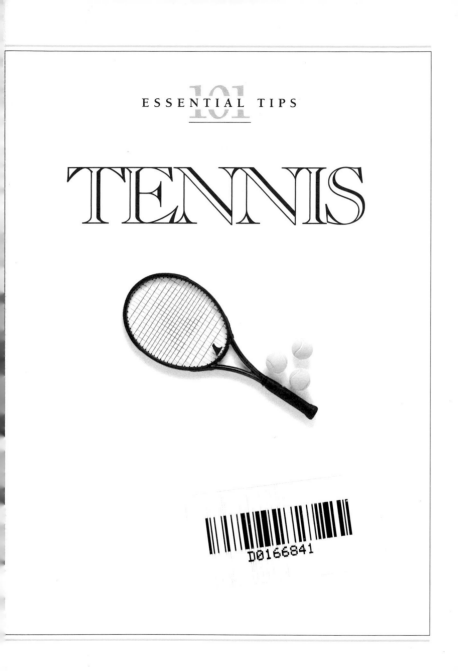

D0166841

ESSENTIAL TIPS

# TENNIS

Paul Douglas

DK PUBLISHING, INC.

www.dk.com

A DK PUBLISHING BOOK

www.dk.com

**Editor** Simon Adams
**Art Editor** Alison Shackleton
**Series Editor** Charlotte Davies
**Managing Art Editor** Amanda Lunn
**Production Controller** Louise Daly
**US Editor** Laaren Brown

First American Edition, 1995
2 4 6 8 10 9 7 5 3
Published in the United States by
Dorling Kindersley Publishing, Inc.,
95 Madison Avenue,
New York, New York 10016

Distributed by Houghton Mifflin Company, Boston.

ISBN 0-7894-0182-7

Computer page makeup by Alison Shackleton
Text film output in Great Britain by The Right Type
Reproduced by Colourscan, Singapore
Printed and bound by Graphicom, Italy

# ESSENTIAL TIPS

# PREPARING TO PLAY

## 1 WHAT TO WEAR

Choose tennis clothes that are comfortable to wear and made of light, washable fabrics. Shorts and skirts should not be too tight around the waistband, and shirts must allow your shoulders and arms freedom to move. It is advisable to wear socks with cushioned soles and heels for added comfort and protection.

Tennis shirt

Ice pack to reduce swelling

Tennis shorts

Tennis shirt

Hairband to keep hair out of eyes

Ball clip and ball

MEN'S TENNIS CLOTHES

Cushioned socks

Wristband to keep palm dry

Tennis skirt

WOMEN'S TENNIS CLOTHES

Cushioned socks to protect feet

**ELASTIC BANDAGE**
*A flexible bandage provides warmth and support for a strained elbow.*

# 2 SHOES

Protect your feet and improve your footwork on the court by choosing good tennis shoes. They must provide flexibility and stability and give support to your insteps, ankles, and Achilles tendons.

Ideally, you should select shoes that suit your game and the type of court on which you play most often. Different court surfaces require different soles: smooth soles for indoors, spiked for grass, and herringbone for general use. If you can only afford one pair of shoes, cross-trainers are good because they can be used for almost any sport.

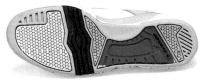

**ALL-PURPOSE SHOE**
*This tennis shoe has a multipurpose sole that allows the player to perform well on grass, clay, or asphalt surfaces.*

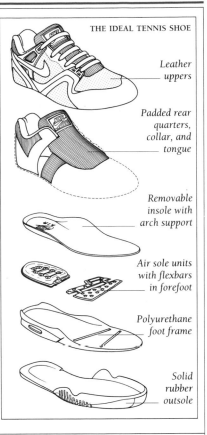

THE IDEAL TENNIS SHOE

*Leather uppers*

*Padded rear quarters, collar, and tongue*

*Removable insole with arch support*

*Air sole units with flexbars in forefoot*

*Polyurethane foot frame*

*Solid rubber outsole*

# 3 WHICH TENNIS BALLS?

Tennis balls have to undergo rigorous testing procedures before they are approved for tournament play. Always choose leading brand balls that are sold in pressurized cans, because it is bad for your game to play with inferior tennis balls. If you are practicing with a partner or working out using a ball machine however, second-grade balls are acceptable.

**TENNIS BALLS**

# 4 CHOOSING THE RIGHT RACQUET

Racquets come in many different shapes and sizes. Most are variations on the oversized head type. These racquets are light and strong, and more powerful than slimmer-bodied models. Their streamlined heads and broad dimensions guarantee better maneuverability and stiffness. When buying a new racquet, choose one that feels right for your grip. Beginners might want a cheaper model before buying a powerful frame.

**MATERIALS**
*The days of wooden racquets are over. Modern racquets are made of Kevlar, boron, and fiberglass, combining flexibility with strength. Powerful players require stiffer frames than touch players.*

*Carrying case to protect racquet*

*Racquet head*

*Shoulders link head to the shaft*

*Shaft disperses vibration from the head*

*Handle is often padded for protection*

**OVERGRIP**
*Wind an overgrip diagonally up the handle to provide more feel in the racquet.*

RACQUET STRINGS

# 5 WHICH STRINGS?

Racquet strings must be woven in a uniform pattern in the racquet frame to guarantee a flat hitting surface. There are two basic types of synthetic strings – monofilament and multifilament. Multifilament strings are generally superior.

# 6 IMPROVING YOUR BALL CONTROL

Practice altering the angle of the racquet face for different shots when hitting the ball by bouncing the ball up off the strings, then flipping the racquet head over so that the next bounce comes off the other surface. A more difficult exercise is to bounce the ball off the edge of the racquet. Both drills develop control and strengthen your wrist.

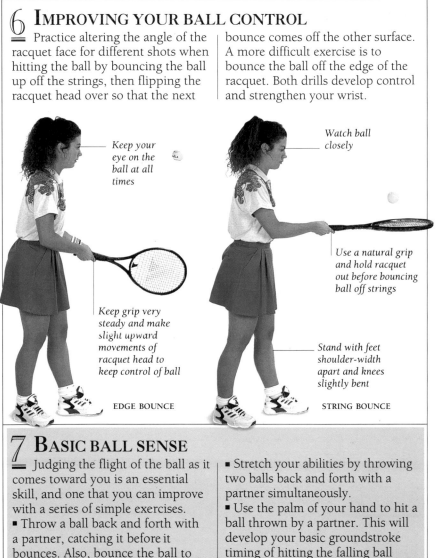

*Keep your eye on the ball at all times*

*Keep grip very steady and make slight upward movements of racquet head to keep control of ball*

**EDGE BOUNCE**

*Watch ball closely*

*Use a natural grip and hold racquet out before bouncing ball off strings*

*Stand with feet shoulder-width apart and knees slightly bent*

**STRING BOUNCE**

# 7 BASIC BALL SENSE

Judging the flight of the ball as it comes toward you is an essential skill, and one that you can improve with a series of simple exercises.

■ Throw a ball back and forth with a partner, catching it before it bounces. Also, bounce the ball to each other and catch it.

■ Stretch your abilities by throwing two balls back and forth with a partner simultaneously.

■ Use the palm of your hand to hit a ball thrown by a partner. This will develop your basic groundstroke timing of hitting the falling ball between knee and waist height.

# 8 JOGGING & STRETCHING

Warm up before you play. It helps avoid injury, makes you feel mentally more like playing, and improves your performance. Begin with a gentle jog to raise your pulse rate. Then spend 10 to 20 seconds on each exercise, first on one leg or side, then the other, as appropriate. Take it easy and enjoy the warm-up. Go through the routine again, holding each stretch slightly longer. Playing requires dynamic movement, so always jog and stretch first. Spend 15 minutes warming up.

*Keep shoulders relaxed*

*Let arms hang loose*

*Flex legs and take small steps*

1 Slowly jog around the court up to five times to warm up your body. On the last two laps, add side-skips and running backward.

*Rest head on arms if you wish*

*Stand about 1 ft (30 cm) from wall and lean toward it*

*Keep legs flat on the ground*

4 Stretch your middle and lower leg by leaning against a wall with your right leg stretched backward. Move your hips forward and stretch.

5 To stretch your stomach muscles, lie flat on your stomach with your arms straight out in front of you. Pull yourself upright onto your palms.

*Keep your right leg extended backward*

*As you raise and lower hips, press body weight forward*

*Pull hips forward and heel in tight toward buttocks*

*Keep left leg straight to support body weight as you bend right knee*

2 To stretch your upper leg, take a step forward with your left leg, bending your knee and keeping it above your ankle. Lower hips and press forward.

3 Stretch your front upper leg by placing your left palm against a wall, bending your right knee, and gripping your foot with your right hand.

*Keep back horizontal*

*Place left elbow outside and above right knee to stop body from twisting back*

*Rest right hand behind you*

*Keep left leg straight*

6 To stretch your arms and wrists, place your hands on the floor with your fingers pointing toward your knees with your thumbs outside.

7 Stretch your body by putting your left leg on the ground and your right foot behind your left knee. Turn and look over your right shoulder.

# 9 FIT FOR TENNIS

For strength and general fitness, follow a routine of body resistance exercises. For stamina, run at a steady pace for half a mile (a kilometer) every other day.

Gradually run faster and increase your distance. Speed is vital too, so do some sprints on the court, running between the sidelines. For flexibility, do your daily warm-up.

*Hold for a second or two and then lower gently*

*Keep knees slightly bent*

*Keep head up and shoulders back*

*Use arms to balance yourself*

*Keep legs slightly bent*

*As you leap, pull knees up sharply toward chest*

**BUDDY TRAINING**
*Try this exercise with a partner. Stand back-to-back and interlock arms at the elbow. Then bend your knees, bend forward from the waist, and lift your partner onto your back. Buddy exercises build strength.*

1 For a double knee jump, stand with your feet together. Crouch down and then leap into the air, bringing your knees up to your chest.

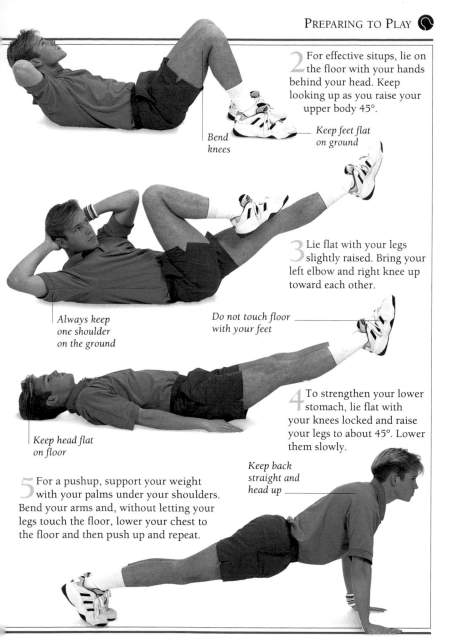

2 For effective situps, lie on the floor with your hands behind your head. Keep looking up as you raise your upper body 45°.

*Bend knees*

*Keep feet flat on ground*

3 Lie flat with your legs slightly raised. Bring your left elbow and right knee up toward each other.

*Always keep one shoulder on the ground*

*Do not touch floor with your feet*

4 To strengthen your lower stomach, lie flat with your knees locked and raise your legs to about 45°. Lower them slowly.

*Keep head flat on floor*

*Keep back straight and head up*

5 For a pushup, support your weight with your palms under your shoulders. Bend your arms and, without letting your legs touch the floor, lower your chest to the floor and then push up and repeat.

# ON THE COURT

## 10 THE COURT

You need to know the court, its markings, surfaces, and net in order to get the best out of a game of tennis. Tennis lines are boundary lines and are named according to their function. The baselines and sidelines limit the depth and width of your drives and volleys, while the service lines restrict the depth of your service.

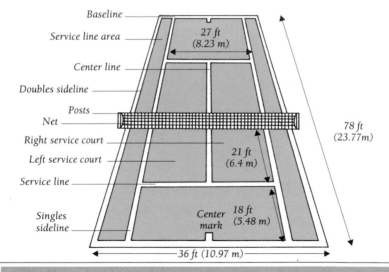

Baseline

Service line area — 27 ft (8.23 m)

Center line

Doubles sideline

Posts

Net

Right service court

Left service court — 21 ft (6.4 m)

Service line

78 ft (23.77m)

Singles sideline

Center mark — 18 ft (5.48 m)

36 ft (10.97 m)

## 11 COURT SURFACES

There are four main court surfaces. Each of them produces different conditions of play and has a marked effect on your game. Experience will teach you which one you prefer.
■ Grass is a fast playing surface but is hard to maintain; artificial grass can be either fast or slow.
■ Clay produces a slow game.
■ Cement results in a fast or slow game, depending on its texture.
■ Asphalt is slow but plays faster when the surface is painted.

# 12 THE NET

The net is more than just a barrier strung across the middle of the court: it also dictates your stroke play and the type of shot you play. It provides problems for every shot. Your task is to find the best solution that will get the ball over the net and place it where it may force a weak return or win the point outright. Your opponent has similar problems to solve.

**NET DICTATES PLAY**
*Because the net is 6 in (16 cm) lower in the center than at the posts, play most shots over the middle of the net.*

*Post is 3 ft 6 in (1.07 m) high and 3 ft (0.91 m) outside doubles sideline*

*Center is 3 ft (0.91 m) high*

*Singles post is 3 ft (0.91 m) outside singles sideline*

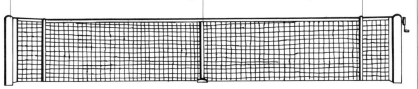

THE TENNIS NET

# 13 MENTAL SKILLS

Tennis is not just a game of physical ability, techniques, and tactics. As you gain experience, you will discover that 75 percent of the game is in the mind. Develop these skills to help your game:
▪ Concentration: Learn to focus your attention like a champion.
▪ Self-belief: Build up your self-confidence by visualizing success.
▪ Motivation: The extent of your desire to play and succeed is the measure of the progress you make.

# 14 MENTAL TRAINING

You can improve your mental skills with mind-training exercises in the same way as you practice to improve your game.
▪ Visualize yourself as a calm player in control of your game, and repeat a short phrase to inspire confidence.
▪ Set yourself goals to increase your motivation. Make them challenging, attainable, and performance-related.
▪ Practice concentrating – on your opponent's serve, or on the height of the ball as it crosses the net.

# 15 HOW THE BALL TRAVELS

When you first play ground-strokes, anticipating the flight of the ball after it bounces can be difficult. Judge where the ball will bounce on your side of the court, but avoid rushing toward it. Position yourself behind, and a comfortable distance from, the bounce point in order to control your return. The service has two flights; the volley only one.

**THE FLIGHT OF THE BALL**
*A ball has two flights: the first as it leaves your opponent's racket, the second after it bounces on your side of the net.*

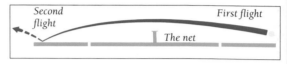

Second flight

First flight

The net

# 16 THE READY POSITION

To return the ball well you need good judgment and effective receiving skills. To develop these, start from an alert and stable ready position. Face the net with your weight on the balls of your feet and your racquet held centrally in order to allow easy play on either side of your body.

*Watch your opponent play the ball to anticipate its speed and direction*

*Support racquet head by lightly holding it at the throat*

*Stand with feet shoulder-width apart for stability and with knees bent to lower your center of gravity*

**FROM THE SIDE**
*Bend to get your eyes in line with the shot. Keep your elbows away from your body for freedom of movement.*

# 17 WHEN TO HIT THE BALL

You must know exactly when and where your racquet head should make contact with the ball. This will enable you to position your body in relation to the ball to ensure perfect timing and control.
- For groundstrokes, play the ball between knee and waist height. When serving, hit the falling ball with your racquet arm extended overhead. For volleys, hit the ball between waist and shoulder height.
- While a drive or service is played at a racquet-arm's distance, a volley is played closer to the body.
- In relation to your body, the ball should be opposite your leading hip for forehand, ahead of your leading hip for backhand, and in front of you for both volleys and services.

*Elbow and wrist joints extend racquet arm and add to speed of racquet head at impact*

# 18 BIOMECHANICS

Biomechanics is simply the study of human motion. It is based on three main principles – the use of joints, stability, and each action having a reaction. Momentum, both straight and rotational, will help you play a powerful, controlled game of tennis.

*Shoulder power adds vertical thrust as racquet arm extends*

*Free arm counterbalances playing arm*

*Shoulders unwind to deliver force against ball*

*Left arm reacts against rotational energy to direct force upward*

*Action and reaction initiate momentum and build up force through legs*

*Front foot delivers momentum, which transfers up through legs to body*

# 19 THE IMPORTANCE OF YOUR GRIP

How you hold the racquet determines how you play the game. The feel you get from the ball after it hits your racket is communicated to you through your grip.

- The basic grip is the Eastern Forehand grip. "Shake hands" with your racquet, with your palm behind the handle, for a comfortable grip that gives you maximum strength to hit an approaching ball.
- As your play becomes more advanced, you may require different grips. These will be introduced to you with each new stroke you learn.

**EASTERN FOREHAND GRIP**

# 20 HOW THE BALL HITS THE RACQUET

The angle of your racquet face to the ball has a direct bearing on the outcome of any shot. The ball stays on your strings for about five-thousandths of a second and goes exactly where your racquet's strings are aiming. For almost every shot, you should keep your racquet face within five degrees of the vertical (lob and drop shots excepted).

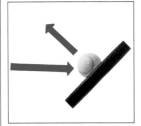

**OPEN FACE**
*An open racquet face plays the ball upward and encourages it to spin backward.*

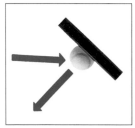

**CLOSED FACE**
*A closed racquet face plays the ball downward and encourages it to spin forward.*

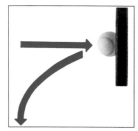

**FLAT FACE**
*A flat racquet face plays the ball straight ahead before gravity pulls it downward.*

# 21 USING SPIN

Spin, the way a ball rotates, has a considerable effect on how a ball travels through the air and bounces. The spin itself will be affected by whether the ball bounces off the court or your racquet strings. Experiment with the three types of spin and see how each one affects a shot.

*When serving with a slice, angle racquet face slightly and hit up and across back of ball from right to left to produce right-hand sidespin*

**SLICE SERVICE**

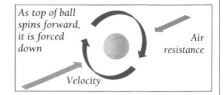

*As top of ball spins forward, it is forced down*

*Air resistance*

*Velocity*

**TOPSPIN**
*When you play topspin shots, aim higher over the net than you would when playing a basic drive.*

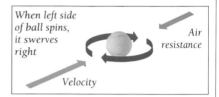

*When left side of ball spins, it swerves right*

*Air resistance*

*Velocity*

**SIDESPIN**
*Sidespin is used for slice serving. Combined with topspin, it produces the topspin serve that kicks and swerves.*

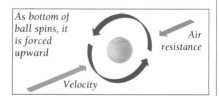

*As bottom of ball spins, it is forced upward*

*Air resistance*

*Velocity*

**UNDERSPIN**
*Lobbing apart, underspin shots travel low over the net. Underspin can be combined with sidespin in approach shot play.*

# 22 DOUBLE-COLORED BALLS

To recognize easily which type of spin you have applied, try practicing with double-colored balls. Note the effect that each type of spin has on the flight of the ball.

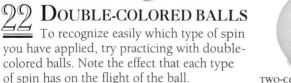

**TWO-COLOR BALLS**

# 23 CALLING THE SHOTS

A stroke is the action of hitting the ball, while a shot describes the flight and eventual destination of the ball after impact. Many tennis shots can be produced from different strokes, and it is worthwhile learning them in order to improve your game. Playing different shots makes for a more enjoyable game by allowing you to use different tactics.

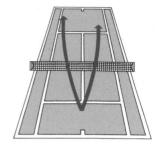

**APPROACH SHOT**
*Play this groundstroke to any part of the court as you approach the net to volley.*

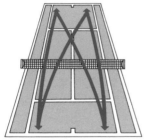

**CROSSCOURT AND DOWN-THE-LINE**
*Employ either shot to keep your opponent on the run and pinned in the backcourt.*

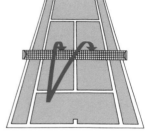

**DROP SHOT**
*Usually underspun, the drop shot should land just over the net with little bounce.*

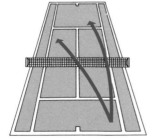

**PASSING SHOT**
*Passing shots don't need depth; just hit them past your advancing opponent.*

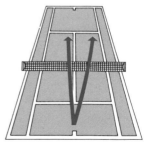

**CHIP SHOT**
*Chip the ball at your opponent's feet or angle it past him as he approaches the net.*

# THE FOREHAND

## 24 THE PERFECT FOREHAND

The key to a perfect forehand is to develop an aggressive approach from the beginning. If you have an urge to attack the ball on the forehand side, go for it. The forehand is the major groundstroke for both beginner and advanced player alike and is the most natural groundstroke to use. When using the forehand, develop a flowing movement that allows you to run for your next shot or recover to your previous position.

*After hitting ball, follow its flight with racquet face*

*Begin takeback before reaching hitting area*

*Turn sideways and set off on either foot, adjusting footwork as you go*

*Position yourself parallel to ball's flight and unwind naturally as you step into the ball*

*Let back foot swing through after impact, using it to launch yourself toward next location*

**THE FLIGHT OF THE BALL**
*To hit your forehand deep to the far baseline, aim another net's height (about 3 ft (1 m) over the net.*

# 25 THE BEST FOREHAND GRIP

How you hold the racquet can dictate your method of play. Begin with a natural grip to allow the body to perform smoothly. The most natural grip for the forehand is often the basic Eastern Forehand, but three other grips might suit you better. Racquet handles have planes and slants, so getting the right grip is easy. Grips affect the position of your feet, so adopt the footwork that complements your choice of grip.

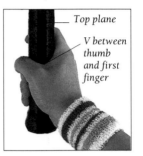

**MODIFIED EASTERN GRIP**
*Place the V between thumb and index finger in the center of the top plane. Place palm behind the handle with your thumb wrapped around.*

**SEMI-WESTERN GRIP**
*Place your V on the upper right slant of the racquet and the knuckle of your index finger on the top edge of the lower right slant.*

**WESTERN GRIP**
*Place your V on the rear plane with your index finger knuckle on the lower right slant. The palm is placed toward the bottom plane.*

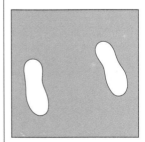

**CLOSED STANCE**
*Turn on your right foot to get sideways to the ball. Now step in almost parallel to the ball's flight with your left foot.*

**SEMI-OPEN STANCE**
*Place your back foot more behind than parallel to ball's flight. Step in more openly, releasing the upper body's rotational momentum.*

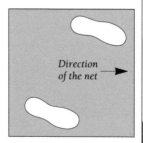

**OPEN STANCE**
*Your back foot positions you and steps in behind the ball simultaneously. Your other foot moves marginally forward to aid balance.*

# 26 THE TAKEBACK

To get ready to hit the ball, turn sideways from the ready position you have already learned, release your nonplaying hand for balance, and bend your knees as you take the racquet back early at the hitting height. At the end of your takeback, relax your elbow and let your racquet head form a natural loop, adding rhythm and speed to provide a positive feeling of lift to your forward swing.

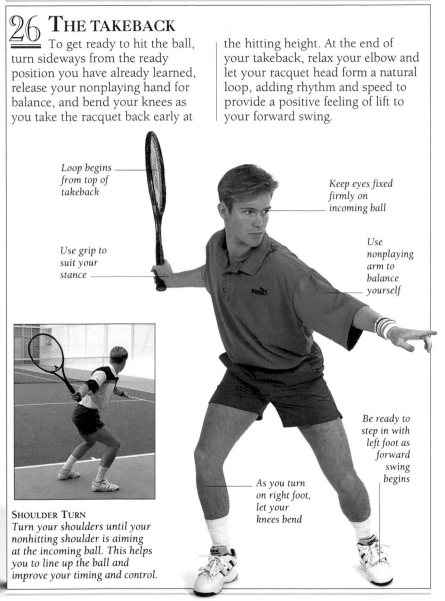

*Loop begins from top of takeback*

*Keep eyes fixed firmly on incoming ball*

*Use grip to suit your stance*

*Use nonplaying arm to balance yourself*

*Be ready to step in with left foot as forward swing begins*

*As you turn on right foot, let your knees bend*

**SHOULDER TURN**
*Turn your shoulders until your nonhitting shoulder is aiming at the incoming ball. This helps you to line up the ball and improve your timing and control.*

# 27 THE HIT

To guarantee a perfect hit every time, step in with your left foot and swing the racquet head up to meet the ball between knee and waist height. Swing the racquet across the hip line from low to high, and extend your arm without locking the elbow. Hitting with a bent elbow means you are too close to the ball. This can result in a loss of control over your shot.

*Keep head steady and eyes on the ball*

*Swing right shoulder powerfully into the hit*

*Squeeze your grip and keep racquet face almost vertical*

*Transfer weight forward over bending left knee to create sound hitting platform*

**RACQUET-ARM'S DISTANCE**
*Swing out comfortably to racquet-arm's distance to the ball at impact to generate full power and control.*

*Keep feet parallel and more than shoulder width apart to provide stability at the hit*

# 28 THE FOLLOWTHROUGH

Once you have hit the ball, don't stop! You need to keep your momentum in order to regain the ready position naturally in time for the next shot. So, after hitting the ball, continue swinging your racquet head through the hitting zone – the general area of the court where you strike the ball – to above head height with a powerful, lifting action. Keep the racquet face steady as it follows the flight of the ball.

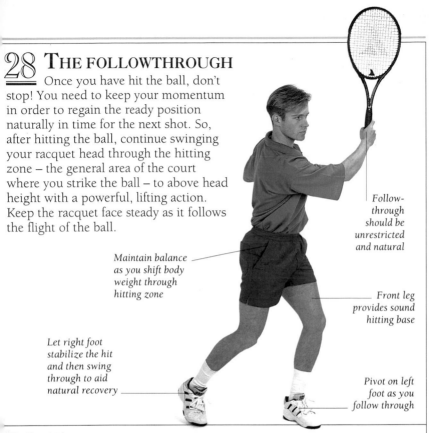

*Follow-through should be unrestricted and natural*

*Maintain balance as you shift body weight through hitting zone*

*Front leg provides sound hitting base*

*Let right foot stabilize the hit and then swing through to aid natural recovery*

*Pivot on left foot as you follow through*

# 29 PRACTICING

To improve your forehand, get your partner to drop balls for you to hit over the net. Next, get him to throw balls underhand to you over the net, simulating an opponent's shot, for you to hit back.
■ Then rally from midcourt, hitting crosscourt drives to each other in the diagonally opposite service area.
■ When you can keep a 10-shot rally going, move back until you can rally with each other from behind the baselines. Try a 10-shot rally to begin with, then aim for a 20-shot rally, hitting drives deep into each other's forehand corners and making each ball bounce between the service line and the baseline.
■ Be sure to recover to a central position behind the center mark after each shot, to practice the movements that matchplay requires.

# 30 ATTACKING PLAY

Attack your opponent by playing forehand drives deep into his or her forehand and backhand corners to pin him in the backcourt. Aim your shots crosscourt. When he switches to a down-the-line drive, it will be easier to return the ball in either direction.

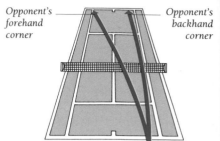

*Opponent's forehand corner*

*Opponent's backhand corner*

# 31 ADDING TOPSPIN

Applying topspin to your forehand drive can put your opponent off guard. It is a useful accessory to your basic forehand attack. Use a full Eastern or a Semi-Western grip. On the takeback, bring the racquet back at about the hitting height and form a deep loop with the racquet head as you join the takeback to the forward swing.

*Keep wrist action freer than for basic drive*

*Use free hand for balance*

*Racquet strings brush steeply up back of ball to impart severe topspin*

*Follow through naturally, letting elbow bend*

**THE TAKEBACK**

*Sweep racquet head through hit from low to high*

**THE HIT**

**THE FOLLOWTHROUGH**

# THE BACKHAND

## 32 THE PERFECT BACKHAND

The key to a perfect backhand is the ability to uncoil into the hit with power. Also, develop the ability to turn and run while at the same time preparing your stroke and getting in the right position in the hitting area. Add this on-the-move drive to your groundstroke play and gain full control in the backcourt.

*Swing from in to out during forward stroke*

*Approach ball to get behind and parallel to its line of flight*

*Good timing relies on perfect footwork and positioning*

*Hit ball between knee and waist height*

## 33 THE BEST GRIP

Use an Eastern Backhand grip for the backhand drive. For this, you place your V in the upper left slant of the racquet handle and your thumb across the rear plane. The knuckle of your index finger is on the upper right slant. Combined with a firm wrist, this grip will help you to develop a powerful, well-controlled backhand drive.

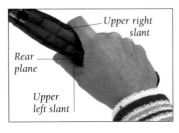

*Upper right slant*

*Rear plane*

*Upper left slant*

**EASTERN BACKHAND GRIP**

29

# 34 THE TAKEBACK

From the ready position, face the net from behind your baseline. Hold the racquet in front, supporting it with your nonplaying hand. Turn your shoulders fully and shift your weight onto your left foot. Keep your support hand on the racquet as you bring it behind your left hip. Complete the takeback with your back facing toward the net. Your weight is ready to be transferred forward as your body uncoils and your right foot steps in.

*Take racquet back before beginning loop*

*Pivot whole body around and try to get hips parallel to flight of ball*

*Look over hitting shoulder at oncoming ball*

*Let knee bend as you turn away to play the shot*

**READY TO HIT**
*As you turn your shoulders, put your weight on your back foot. Your racquet will loop down before swinging up and out.*

## 35 MAKING ROOM TO SWING

It is very important to give yourself plenty of room to swing out and up to meet the ball. Begin the step-in and forward swing at the same time. Joining the back and forward swing with a shallow loop, swing the racquet in a broad sweep from low to high, through the hitting zone. Meet the ball in front of you.

## 36 POWERFUL STROKES

The easy power in the backhand comes from the uncoiling action of your body and playing arm. To deliver power with control, pivot on your back foot and turn your hitting shoulder until your back faces the net. With your racquet prepared behind your rear hip, you are ready to uncoil with power and accuracy.

## 37 THE HIT

Release your support hand from the racquet, and make a shallow loop with the racquet head to guarantee a low-to-high forward swing as you step in. Hit the ball a racquet-arm's distance away in the sideways position. Your grip will give you a feeling of solidity at impact and provide a natural racquet-face angle for lift and direction.

*After releasing support hand from racquet, extend it for balance*

*Hold racquet arm straight at impact with wrist locked*

*Keep racquet face almost vertical but angled slightly to encourage lift*

*Transfer body weight onto bent front knee as you sweep racquet head up to meet the ball*

*Step front foot in parallel to ball's line of flight to guarantee solid hitting platform*

*At end of backhand stroke, racquet arm should be extended in front of you above head height*

*Keep head down until stroke is complete*

## 38 THE FOLLOWTHROUGH

To follow through after hitting the ball, feel your racquet head lifting through the ball in the direction in which you are aiming. Your racquet arm should be straight but not locked out, with your body leaning forward over your bent front knee. As the followthrough ends, let your back foot swing through and recover to the ready position facing the net.

*Keep sideways throughout stroke*

**BUDDY PRACTICE**
*With a partner, practice swapping backhand drives crosscourt. Start with a 10-shot rally, then progress to a 20-shot or even 30-shot rally. If you find rallying difficult, drop balls for each other to hit, or feed them by hand or from your racquet to your partner.*

*Back foot in contact with court to add balance to followthrough*

## 39 PROBLEM SHOTS

If the ball is coming directly at you, step away from its flight path with your front foot. As you transfer your weight onto this foot, lean away from the ball and fully extend your racquet arm at the hit. With a high ball, take your racquet back higher than you would for a basic drive. Bring your racquet up to meet the ball with the full racquet face.

# 40 BACKHAND DROP

The backhand drop shot is an advanced touch stroke and requires diligent practice. Take your racquet back to about head height, with the racquet face angled back slightly to allow underspin to be applied. Push the racquet head down and under the ball and feel the strings gripping the ball. The ball is deflected up and off the strings, dropping over the net with little bounce as the spin takes its effect. The followthrough is short.

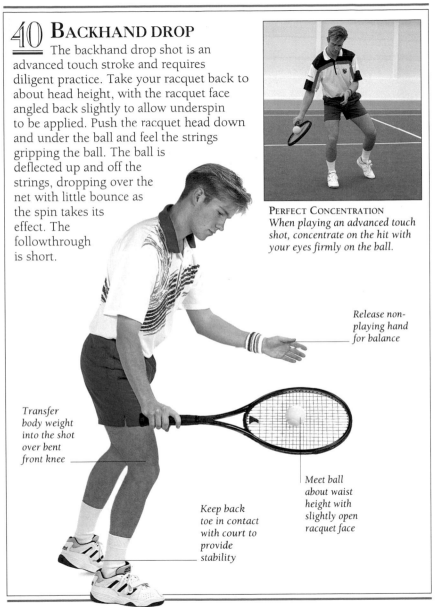

**PERFECT CONCENTRATION**
*When playing an advanced touch shot, concentrate on the hit with your eyes firmly on the ball.*

*Release non-playing hand for balance*

*Transfer body weight into the shot over bent front knee*

*Meet ball about waist height with slightly open racquet face*

*Keep back toe in contact with court to provide stability*

33

# 41 DOUBLE-HANDED BACKHAND

The double-handed backhand is a perfect option for young players who lack physical strength, and for older players just starting out. This powerful, two-handed stroke will encourage you to attack the ball with topspin and provides a feeling of greater strength and control. When gripping the racquet, just add the other hand to begin with, but later on try changing your grip as you begin the takeback.

*Point racquet head downward*

*Let racquet sweep out and up through ball*

1 As you pivot ready to hit the ball, simply add your other hand to the handle and take your racquet back below your intended hitting height.

*Use your back foot for balance*

2 Step in with your right foot, swinging your racquet to meet the ball in front of your leading hip. Your body weight has shifted onto your front foot.

*Finish high for good topspin effect*

*Whip racquet head up with pronounced wrist action to get more topspin on ball*

*Weight fully transferred as legs and body straighten*

3 Allow your body to uncoil fully as you drive through the ball. A firm-wristed drive with a flatter followthrough may provide more pace but less margin for error.

## 42 CHANGING GRIP

As your double-hander improves, position your playing hand with an Eastern Backhand or Continental grip. Support the racquet with your spare hand and turn your playing hand inward. Slide your support hand down to form a left-handed Eastern Forehand grip above your right hand.

**GRIP CHANGE**
*Turn playing hand until V between thumb and index finger is on inner edge of handle.*

**GRIP READY**
*Slide supporting hand down the handle until it nestles in the V of playing hand.*

# THE SERVE

## 43 THE PERFECT SERVE

The serve is the most devastating stroke in tennis. From a static position, a well-timed serve will fire a ball into your opponent's court with deadly precision. For a perfect serve, you should feel momentum rising up through your body as your legs, hips, back, shoulders, playing arm, and wrist create a powerful chain reaction.

*Stand with feet a good distance apart and knees slightly flexed*

*To prepare for the serve, push down into the court with back foot*

*Build power into your serve by using your leg muscles*

*Follow through your serve to give yourself momentum for next shot*

**THE FLIGHT OF THE BALL**
*The ball travels in an arc from the baseline into the service court diagonally opposite. It reaches the far baseline after the bounce.*

# 44 GRIPPING THE BALL

To hold one ball, grasp it with the thumb and four fingers of your nonplaying hand. To hold two, grip the first ball with your thumb and first two fingers, and the second with your third and fourth fingers.

ONE-BALL GRIP          TWO-BALL GRIP

# 45 THE BEST GRIP

When you first serve, try the Eastern or Modified Eastern grip. Graduate to the Continental grip, where the V between thumb and index finger is to the left of the top plane's center, with the index finger knuckle on the upper right slant.

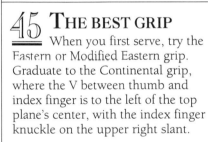

— Upper right slant

Top plane

THE CONTINENTAL GRIP

# 46 SERVING PRACTICE

The serving action is simply an overhand throw. If you can throw a ball overhand, you can serve. With a partner at the far baseline, take turns at throwing a ball over the net to each other.

Make ball
bounce
in diagonally
opposite
service court —

Having bent —
elbow, extend
arm and
release ball

Look up and —
follow ball's
flight

Use left arm
for balance

Stand behind
baseline on
either side of
center mark —

# 47 FOOT FAULTS

There is no point in making a perfect service if, before striking the ball, you step onto or over the baseline with either foot. Your service would be disallowed and you could not take it again. To avoid foot faults, have a wider stance and practice keeping your back foot on the ground for several serves.

**FRONT FOOT FAULT**
*To cure the above foot fault, start with your feet farther apart.*

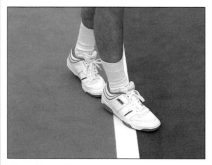

**REAR FOOT FAULT**
*If you throw the ball too far forward, your back foot may swing across the line too soon.*

# 48 THE SERVING STANCE

To prepare to serve, stand behind the baseline within 1 ft 8 in (50 cm) of the center mark. Face your opponent sideways to the net with your feet shoulder-width apart. Slightly bend your knees with your weight poised on your back foot. Point your left toe toward the right-hand net post. Put your weight on your rear foot, ready to be transferred forward as your arms part. Relax your arms and shoulders.

*Study your opponent's position, then focus on ball as you begin to serve*

*Hold balls against racquet strings and point racquet toward service court*

*Push into ground with back foot to get your serve in motion*

# 49 THE TOSS

Toss the ball up in front of you and a little to your right. As you transfer your weight, use your back foot for stability. When you release the ball, bend your racquet arm and lift your racquet until the tip points skyward. At the end of the toss, both arms should point upward.

# 50 THE THROWING POSITION

From the throwing position, don't stop, but feel a pause at the height of the toss. Then let your racquet drop smoothly down into the throwing position, deep between your shoulder blades. Use your trailing leg to stabilize yourself.

*Point racquet head and placing hand up as ball reaches its peak*

*Relax elbow to let racquet head drop into throwing position, keeping racquet clear of body*

*Flex front knee to cushion forward movement of your weight*

*Maintain balance over bent knee prior to hit*

# 51 THE HIT

To hit the ball over the net perfectly each time, straighten your legs and launch the racquet head up. Your body should be fully stretched out at impact, with just your toes on the ground. Extend your racquet arm straight up from the shoulder.

*Hit ball in middle of strings*

*Turn hitting shoulder in powerfully as you throw racquet head up to meet the ball*

*Straighten legs at the hit, with back foot no longer anchored, and ready for followthrough action*

*After impact, toss arm drops away as followthrough begins*

**A FEEL FOR THE BALL**
*In order to improve your accuracy and reduce margin for error over the net, develop the feeling that you are hitting up, through, and over the ball.*

# 52 THE FOLLOWTHROUGH

After impact, allow your racquet to swing down past your left leg in a full followthrough. At the same time, let your right foot swing across the baseline for balance. Finish with your weight on your right foot and with the right knee bent to assist your recovery behind the baseline or your journey forward to volley.

*Let racquet swing past your left side*

*Keep your eye on the ball as you follow through*

# 53 SLICE SERVE

The slice serve is the cutting edge of your serving firepower. Use a slice delivery to swerve the ball sharply through the air before and after the bounce, keeping the ball low as it takes your opponent out of the court. Sidespin makes it safe, so you can use this alternative technique for your second serve.

*Firmly "bite" side of ball with racquet strings*

*Allow shoulders to turn in at hit*

**PLAYING WITH SLICE**
*In order to perfect the slice serve, try to feel your racquet cutting across the right side of the ball at 3 o'clock. Always keep your head steady and eyes focused on the ball.*

# 54 DEVELOPING YOUR SERVE

To maintain tactical advantage in a game, you should aim to get at least 70 percent of your first serves into the court. To achieve this, practice serving at three-quarter rather than full speed. When you can serve wide, straight at the body, or down the center against either right- or left-handed players with equal consistency, you will be good enough to win most of your service games. Aim your serves deep or angle them toward the sidelines.

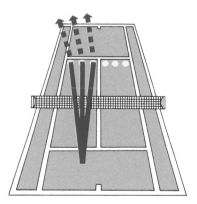

**SERVING AT TARGETS**
*One simple way to develop your serve is to practice serving at targets. Position three targets in your opponent's two serving courts, and then serve two balls at each target. Keep a note of how many serves go in as well as counting how many times you hit a target. As your scores increase, your match play serving should also improve.*

41

# RETURN SERVE

## 55 THE IMPORTANCE OF THE RETURN

The ability to consistently return your opponent's serve affects the outcome of every point, and is second only to the serve in match play importance. It is vital to return every service effectively, but the serving strengths of your opponent govern the type and quality of your reply. Learn to adapt your basic forehand and backhand strokes to counteract the height, speed, spin, and placement of the service.

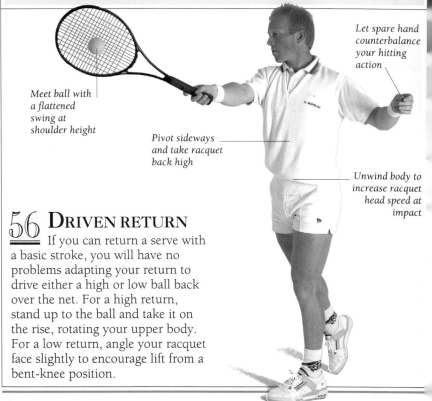

*Let spare hand counterbalance your hitting action*

*Meet ball with a flattened swing at shoulder height*

*Pivot sideways and take racquet back high*

*Unwind body to increase racquet head speed at impact*

## 56 DRIVEN RETURN

If you can return a serve with a basic stroke, you will have no problems adapting your return to drive either a high or low ball back over the net. For a high return, stand up to the ball and take it on the rise, rotating your upper body. For a low return, angle your racquet face slightly to encourage lift from a bent-knee position.

# 57 BLOCKED RETURN

A blocked return is played with a short takeback and a volleylike punch. Stand just inside your baseline and take the ball early. Block or punch through the back of the ball and aim deep to the far baseline to cancel out the server's advantage.

*Use spare arm to balance shot*

*Keep wrist firm and spread index finger for extra control*

*Step across with front foot and punch forward*

**WHEN TO HIT THE BALL**
*When using a blocked return, meet the ball early and out in front of your body.*

# 58 ATTACKING & SURPRISE RETURNS

To respond to a short-length service, take the ball early and hit it down the sideline or crosscourt. The server is unlikely to approach the net behind such a serve, so your attacking return should put him on the defensive and allow you to move upcourt. If the serve is even shorter, angle your return for a winner.

If the server aims deep to your backhand, respond with a topspin lobbed return crosscourt or down the line. It will catch him flatfooted as he moves in.

# 59 LOBBED RETURN

For a lobbed return, move forward inside your baseline and form a short, low takeback before stepping in to sweep your racquet head up the back of the ball to give it heavy topspin. Use your basic Eastern Backhand grip for this shot, playing the return with a firm wrist.

*Keep racquet face almost vertical at impact*

*Stand sideways when playing this shot*

**WHEN TO HIT THE BALL**
*Take a high, bouncing serve on the rise, meeting the ball at about shoulder height.*

*Step into shot and "feel" you are staying longer with the ball*

# 60 RETURN TACTICS

When a service is delivered down the line to your backhand from the right court, move forward inside your baseline and chip your return low at the feet of your opponent. Alternatively, aim toward the sidelines to draw him or her wide and open up the court for you to play a passing shot.

*Aim straight at opponent's feet*

*Move opponent out of position with chip toward sidelines*

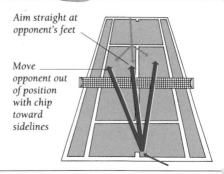

# 61 CHIPPED RETURN

The chipped return is a short, underspun stroke that is useful against spinning or high, bouncing serves. To play this return, move inside your baseline and make a short, high takeback, chipping down through the ball between waist and shoulder height. Keep your racquet with the ball after contact. The ideal chipped return is played wide of, or at the feet of, an incoming volleyer, landing in the opposite service court areas.

*Keep your eyes focused on the ball at impact*

*Tilt racquet face back slightly to apply controlling underspin*

**CHIP AND CHARGE**
*A good alternative use for the chipped return is to use it as an offensive weapon, by chipping the ball deep toward your opponent's baseline and then following it into the net to catch your opponent off guard.*

*Keep feet parallel to or slightly across line of flight of ball*

**WHEN TO HIT THE BALL**
*It is important to meet the ball well in front of your body, with your racquet arm extended, when playing a chipped return.*

45

# THE FOREHAND VOLLEY

## 62 THE PERFECT FOREHAND VOLLEY

The forehand volley is one of the most decisive shots in tennis, and can be the match-winning shot in your game. Play the volley like a boxer's jabbing punch. Advance toward the net and jab your racquet head forward to hit the ball before it bounces. The volley is a short, punched stroke that travels from high to low, compared to the low-to-high swing of the equivalent groundstroke.

*Resist temptation to take a swing at the ball when volleying on the move*

*Always carry racquet in front of you, ready for instant action*

*Split-step in order to anticipate height and direction of incoming ball*

*Keep takeback short for control and play forward for pace*

**THE FLIGHT OF THE BALL**
*In a volley, the ball has only one flight. Try to meet it above net height and aim straight into your opponent's court.*

46

# 63 POSITIONING HANDS & FEET

To begin with, you will feel more confident using the basic Eastern Forehand grip. Place your palm behind the handle and simply "shake hands" with the racquet. As you improve, graduate to the Continental grip you learned for service for greater flexibility. Spread your index finger away from the rest to give an increased feel for the ball.

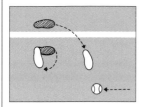

**EASY BALL**
*To return an easy ball, turn on your right foot and step forward with your left foot, parallel to ball's line of flight.*

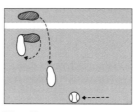

**WIDE BALL**
*To hit a wide ball, pivot to your right and step well across with left foot. Rotate upper body for balance.*

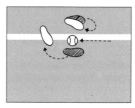

**BODYLINE BALL**
*Pivot on left foot and then step back with your right to get sideways before leaning weight forward.*

# 64 GRABBING THE BALL

The forehand volley action is just like catching the ball with your playing hand, and you can improve your forehand volley with this simple exercise. Stand on the opposite side of the net to your partner, about 10 ft (3 m) back. Ask your partner to throw you a ball underhanded at shoulder height. Reach forward and firmly grab the ball to the side and in front of you before it starts to fall toward the ground. Focus on the ball and "stop" it with your eyes as you make the grab. Now throw the ball back for your partner to grab.

*Always use spare hand to counterbalance your movements*

*Step forward and across as you reach out to grab ball, stabilizing movement with back foot*

*Point released left hand toward oncoming ball*

*Keep wrist firm*

## 65 THE TURN

To prepare to volley the incoming ball, pivot to your right until your racquet is level with your right shoulder. Release your left hand from the racquet throat as you turn and keep your weight on your right foot. Keep your takeback short, getting your racquet head behind the ball and slightly above your intended hitting height.

■ If you have a tendency to swing too far back, stand with your back to a wall and get your partner to feed some balls to your forehand side. This will restrict your takeback.

*Use left foot to steady your turn, but keep it ready for step-in action*

## 66 VOLLEYER TO VOLLEYER

Develop the accuracy and control of your volley by regularly practicing with a partner. Stand on either side of the net in your respective volley positions. Take turns feeding balls to each other at increasing speeds, progressing to a volley rally. Keep the emphasis on fast footwork when turning and stepping in, quick reactions, and minimum takeback.

**VOLLEY FOR GOALS**
*Compete with your partner by volleying between two balls to score points.*

48

# 67 THE HIT

When playing a volley, punch your racquet head forward to meet the ball in front of your body between waist and shoulder height. Try to play the ball at eye level.

- Develop the accuracy and control of your forehand volley by aiming at a target on a wall. Try to keep a 10-shot or 20-shot rally going.

**GRAB-PUNCH POSITION**
*Meet the ball higher and closer to your body than you would in groundstroke play.*

*Meet ball with full face of racquet strings*

*Straighten racquet arm at the hit as you punch down and through ball*

*Back foot stabilizes movement when weight is launched forward*

*Transfer weight positively as you step into the shot*

# 68 THE FOLLOWTHROUGH

After impact, let your shoulder power through as you complete the shot. Keep your knees bent to maintain good stability and a low center of gravity. The slight downward path of your racquet adds underspin for shot control. Keep the followthrough short.

- From a strong net position, volley deep down the sideline to pin your opponent in the backcourt, or try an angled crosscourt volley to place the ball out of reach.

*Keep head steady and eyes focused on ball*

*With your elbow well away from body, keep racquet arm straight and racquet head at about wrist level*

*After completing stroke, let back foot swing through to aid recovery*

*Maintain solid hitting platform in followthrough*

# 69 LOW FOREHAND VOLLEY

To play a low volley well, crouch down and bend your knees. Keep your wrist firm and your racquet head level. Move into your volley by stepping forward and across with your front foot.

*Use free arm for balance*

*Angle racquet face slightly to apply some underspin*

## 70 HIGH FOREHAND VOLLEY

In order to play a good, high forehand volley, you must position yourself sideways; otherwise, you may pull the ball down into the net or play it wide of the sidelines. Take the racquet a little farther back and higher than for the basic volley. Then step in with your left foot, punching the racquet head down and through the ball. Follow through with the racquet head in the direction of the shot.

▪ High volleys need strong arms to punch the ball powerfully at shoulder height, so good fitness is required for this shot.

*Use free arm for balance*

*Keep wrist firm and racquet head up*

*Keep both feet on ground*

## 71 FOREHAND HALF-VOLLEY

A half-volley is an advanced stroke played immediately after the ball has bounced. The takeback must be short and low, with the racquet head at wrist level. Let your knees bend as you turn on your rear foot and get down low with your front foot forward and your back knee close to the ground. Meet the ball just after the bounce, keeping your wrist firm.

*Use left arm for balance*

*Get wrist and racquet head in line*

51

# THE BACKHAND VOLLEY

## 72 THE PERFECT BACKHAND VOLLEY

You may find that the backhand volley is easier to play than its forehand counterpart, because when you take up the sideways position, your playing arm leads the way and encourages positive action. Develop both your backhand and forehand volley sequences by starting from farther back and then moving in quickly to volley.

*Always have racquet ready to make your forward play*

*Keep your eyes on ball all the way through shot*

*Release nonplaying hand as you punch racquet head down through back of ball*

*Keep feet well apart and body well balanced*

**THE FLIGHT OF THE BALL**
*As in the forehand volley, the ball has only one flight. Meet it above net height and aim into opponent's court.*

## 73 THE TURN

Turn sideways to the ball from your ready position and take your racquet back above hitting height, about level with your left shoulder. Support the racquet at the throat with your nonplaying hand. Bend your knees slightly, with your back foot forming a firm base for hitting. For low balls, bend your knees more.

*Keep wrist firm in Eastern Backhand grip*

*Weight poised on back leg will be transferred to front foot at the hit*

## 74 THE HIT

Releasing your left hand, step forward and across slightly with your right foot. Punch your racquet head forward and down through the back of the ball, meeting it between waist and shoulder height with the full face of your racquet strings. As you hit the ball, transfer your weight fully over your bent front knee. Try to keep your feet parallel to, or slightly across, the line of the ball's flight.

*Release left hand to aid balance*

*Keep racquet face steady at hit*

# 75 THE FOLLOWTHROUGH

Let your racquet head follow through a short distance to finish the hitting zone, extending your racquet arm as you play through the ball. The slightly downward action of the racquet, with its bottom edge leading, will apply some underspin to the ball for added control. Control your step-in to stay with the ball in the followthrough.

Keep your eyes focused firmly on ball

Left hand out for balance

Extend playing arm with wrist locked and keep racquet face steady

Lean whole body forward as you play through the ball

**SHOULDER TURN**
Avoid getting caught flat-footed at the net, pulling the ball down. Get your hitting shoulder well around toward the net as you pivot sideways to the oncoming ball.

Keep feet apart to aid stability and lower your center of gravity

# 76 WALL WORK

Volley against a practice wall to improve your stroke. Stand 6 ft (2 m) away: this shortens your stroke and improves your racquet-head control. Start from a sideways position, returning to your ready position between each volley. Keep a 10- or 20-shot rally going to begin with and then aim for a target on the wall to develop greater accuracy.

# 77 VOLLEY TACTICS

Volley the ball deep into the corners of your opponent's court, especially from the midcourt area. When you move in closer there will be opportunities to play angled volleys. Aim to volley straight most of the time, remembering that when you do volley crosscourt, you must be decisive as it opens up a down-the-line shot for your opponent.

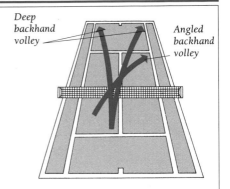

*Deep backhand volley*

*Angled backhand volley*

# 78 BACKHAND HALF-VOLLEY

Like its forehand counterpart, the backhand half-volley is an advanced touch stroke and needs delicate timing. Play your half-volley about midcourt if your approach to the net is too slow. Bend your knees as you turn to make the shot, and step in to play forward from a short takeback. Meet the ball just after the bounce with a lifting motion.

*Keep back fairly straight as you bend low*

*Keep your eyes focused firmly on ball*

*Keep wrist firm*

**LOW BACKHAND VOLLEY**
*Bend low and step forward and across, with your racquet face angled as you punch under the ball just before it bounces.*

*Racquet head vertical or slightly tilted at wrist level*

# LOB & SMASH

## 79 THE PERFECT LOB

A lob is a ball sent high in the air. It requires a fuller stroke than the drive, with a lower takeback and higher finish. It is not just a defensive stroke, because if you have enough speed combined with good racquet control at impact, your perfectly measured lob can instantly turn defense into attack.

*Move off diagonally to intercept ball shortly after bounce*

*Racquet face angled back for underspin*

*Use basic Eastern Backhand or Continental grip for this advanced backhand lob*

*Get down to make shot, with legs wide apart and a low center of gravity*

*To hit ball with underspin, hold racquet with a short, high takeback*

**THE FLIGHT OF THE BALL**
*The basic lob carries a little topspin and should travel in an even arc, clearing the net by about 22 ft (7 m) to land just inside the opposite baseline. The second flight after the bounce should be fairly high.*

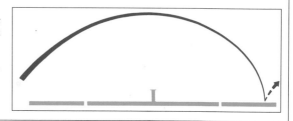

# 80 THE TAKEBACK

Begin your basic lob like a drive, taking your racquet back as you turn sideways. Relax your elbow at the end of the takeback, letting your racquet form a low loop. Step in and start to swing the racquet head forward in a steep upward path.

*Point left hand toward ball to help you balance*

*Use Eastern Forehand grip and keep racquet face open*

*Step in onto bent front knee as you begin the forward swing from the takeback*

**WHEN TO LOB**
*The lob can be a good attacking stroke. Drop a lob behind your opponent and close in as he scampers back on the defense, or use one early in the rally to play havoc with his confidence.*

# 81 LOB TACTICS

Generally, lob deep as short lobs are snapped up by net players. Lob over your opponent's nonplaying shoulder to his backhand corner because a smash is difficult to play if you have to move diagonally backward to reach the ball. Play the basic backhand lob with a degree of topspin to make the ball bounce away from your opponent.

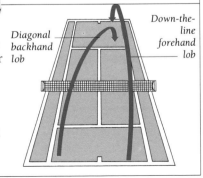

*Diagonal backhand lob*

*Down-the-line forehand lob*

**HIGH FOLLOWTHROUGH**
*After impact, let your racquet swing up through the hitting zone to finish above your head.*

# 82 THE HIT

Leading with the bottom edge of your racquet face, let the racquet swing forward in a steep, upward path to meet the ball in front of your leading hip. Squeeze your grip at impact to steady your wrist, and time your swing to meet the ball between knee and waist height as it falls. You can lob off either foot and vary the height and depth of your lob if your hitting platform is sound.

*Keep head steady and eyes on ball*

*Bring left hand back to act as stabilizer as you turn into the hit*

*Keep racquet face angled back for lift, but not too much or lob will fall short*

*Bent knee aiding lift will straighten as followthrough develops*

# 83 THE PERFECT SMASH

The jump smash epitomizes on-the-move action; it overcomes any lack of reach you might have and deals effectively with deep lobs. To play the shot well, develop both speed and agility to move backward in a sideways position, and power in your legs for leaping high in the air. Use the sidestep or crossover for your run back.

**THE FLIGHT OF THE BALL**
*From close in at the net (A), angle your smash to make it bounce over your opponent's head. From farther back (B), smash the ball deep.*

*Let your right leg swing past left in scissorlike action when you hit ball*

*Meet ball above and in front of you at full racquet-arm's reach*

*After hitting up and over ball, land on left foot*

*Once airborne, drop racquet head into throwing position*

*Jump off back leg to smash ball before it dips behind you*

# 84 FOOTWORK

To line up smashes quickly, you need to keep sideways to the ball as you position yourself behind and below the ball. Both the sidestep and the crossover will get you in the right position. Footwork for the sidestep is simple, but the crossover requires practice.

**SIDESTEP**          **CROSSOVER**

# 85 THE POINT-UP

Pivot sideways, bending your elbow to lift the racquet head as you extend your other arm to point up at your opponent's lob. Keep pointing up as you position yourself to smash the ball. By pointing up longer you will be able to time your smash perfectly.

■ Your left arm plays a vital role; not only does it help you to keep the ball in front of you as you track back, but it also measures half the distance your racquet arm can reach.

*Straighten left arm and point up at falling ball*

*Look along arm at ball*

*Keep elbow high and racquet poised to drop into throwing position*

*Place feet shoulder-width apart for stability*

**OVERHEAD VIEW**
*Point up at the ball as you turn, bringing the racquet in across your shoulders before dropping it deep into the throwing position.*

# 86 THE HIT

Fully extend your racquet arm as you throw your racquet head up to meet the ball, with the full face of the racquet strings. Hit the ball in front of you and finish the stroke like the serve. Your back foot will stabilize you at impact. Start with the Modified Eastern grip and progress as you gain experience to the Continental grip.

*Hit ball ahead of you at racquet-arm's reach*

*Turn playing shoulder powerfully into the hit*

*Stretch and tilt whole body*

*Balance your body with weight forward and legs straight*

*Be on tiptoes at impact*

**FULL STRETCH**
*In action at full stretch, the player meets the ball in front of him. As in serving, the left arm helps to direct force upward.*

# 87 SMASH TACTICS

The smash can only be used against lobs or high-bouncing balls, so develop an attacking game that forces your opponent to put up a defensive lob. Aim for his backhand corner. High lobs should be smashed after the bounce, but use a jump-smash for balls you would not otherwise reach. Inside the service line, angle smashes to the sidelines.

# APPROACH PLAY

## 88 APPROACH SHOTS

In approaching the net, the placement of your shots is crucial to the success of any attack. Allow your position and the height at which you play the ball to dictate the stroke, but shorten the takeback for extra control. Once in the forecourt, use your volleying skills.

*Keep alert and balanced*

1 Play this topspin approach shot with a steep, upward swing. Take the ball early and meet it out in front.

*Step quickly into the shot with either parallel or semi-open footwork*

2 ◁ Follow the line of your approach shot in and then split-step as your opponent makes his play.

*Use underspin on low first volleys*

3 ▷ Having approached the net, volley well by getting your weight forward into the hit and keeping your body steady at impact.

# 89 APPROACH TACTICS

The basic rule of approach tactics is never to approach the net from a deep position. Aim to get where you want to be before your opponent strikes. If this is not possible, then split-step early. The court on the right shows the areas of play. The dark blue area is advisable, the midblue possible, but it is too risky to make an approach shot from the pale blue area. It is much better to retreat behind the baseline and wait for a real opportunity to present itself.

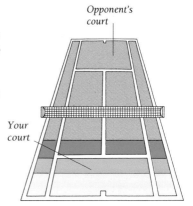

*Opponent's court*

*Your court*

# 90 SPLIT-STEPPING OPTIONS

Split-stepping is simply interrupting your forward run by planting your feet shoulder-width apart in order to gain a mobile ready position. Split-step early in order to be perfectly balanced for instant lateral movement to respond to your opponent's return shot. By split-stepping, you can read that shot and be better able to move quickly to your right to cut off your opponent's crosscourt return, or to your left to backhand volley an attempted passing shot down the line.

*Step to right and punch the ball*

*React and move in response to opponent's shot*

*Step to left to meet ball in front*

**FOREHAND RESPONSE**

**READY POSITION**

**BACKHAND RESPONSE**

*Cut around
right side of
ball to apply
slice to serve*

# $\underline{91}$ SERVING & VOLLEYING

The serve-and-volley is a decisive tactic that can give you control of the net area. As with approach shots, it is accuracy, pace, and depth of service that dictate subsequent volleying success. Give yourself time to reach a good volleying position by serving at three-quarters' speed to your opponent's weaker stroke, applying slice for extra control. Serve-and-volley success relies heavily on basic volleying techniques, so always focus on the ball, react early, and play forward, getting your weight behind every shot.

1 Take up your service stance and select your service type and direction.

*Keep wrist firm
and racquet at
wrist level*

3 △ After split-stepping, get well down, stepping across and settling in for those low first volleys.

2 ◁ Try to cross the service line before split-stepping as your opponent makes his play.

*Split-step
early and be
ready to move
laterally*

# THE GAME OF TENNIS

## 92 RULES OF THE GAME

Always play tennis by the rules. Toss a coin to decide who serves first. Serve from behind your baseline, starting in the right court for the first point, the left for the second. The service ball must be struck before it bounces and must go over the net and land in the diagonally opposite service court. If you serve a fault you can serve again, but a double-fault gives your opponent the point. A receiver cannot volley the serve or let it bounce twice.

**THE UMPIRE**
*The umpire sits in a high chair above the court to see that fair play and the rules of the game are observed.*

## 93 PROGRESSIVE PLAYING

First and foremost, tennis is a game of control. It also requires consistency, depth, and power.

- Develop control by improving your tracking or receiving skills, so that you can move quickly and position yourself correctly in order to time the ball perfectly, whether it is a simple return or the best shot you will ever play in your life!
- As your timing improves, try to be more consistent by not making unforced errors.
- After consistency, depth of shot must be added to your repertoire to keep your opponent away from the net and pinned in the backcourt.
- Finally, in order to dictate or counter your opponent's attack, bring power to your play by developing increased momentum through biomechanical principles.

# 94 TACTICS ON COURT

Tactically, the area behind and up to your baseline is the backcourt, the area on the court between your service line and the net is the forecourt, and the area in between is no-man's-land. If you have to play a shot in no-man's-land, play it and get out fast or you may be caught with the ball at your feet and no time to play the next shot.

▪ Your main tactical aims are to keep the ball in play, to make your opponent run, to wrong-foot your opponent by disguising your intentions, and to play on his or her weaknesses by varying each shot.

CENTERPOINT TACTIC
*Having reached a safe centerpoint in the forecourt, the attacking player moves out to cut off an attempted pass with a low volley.*

# 95 CENTERPOINT AWARENESS

The centerpoint is midway between the two extremes of your opponent's return. It is a good tactic to guarantee that your next centerpoint is close to you, but there is a danger of being caught out on your way there. This need not happen if you ease up when your opponent is playing the ball. In this example, the server plays a wide service to the receiver, who replies with a deep crosscourt return (red) so that his next centerpoint is between the server's possible shots (blue). If the receiver had chosen to play down the line, his next centerpoint would have been well beyond the center mark.

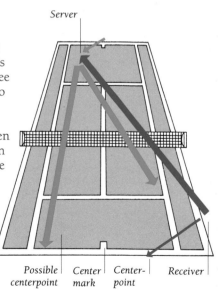

Server

Possible centerpoint | Center mark | Center-point | Receiver

# 96 PERCENTAGE PLAY

Percentage play is about playing the safest shots that provide you with the greatest margin for error. As the court is longer diagonally and the net lower in the middle, it makes sense to hit most shots crosscourt with height and depth. Tactically, choose the shot that is easiest for you to play, even if you've already played it five times in that rally. Your opponent may become impatient and attempt the more difficult down-the-line shot on the next ball.

# 97 PLAYING DOUBLES

In contrast to the singles game, doubles is about teamwork, and you must play together. Try to play level with your partner, aiming to get to the net quickly and remain there until you have won the point. If you are in doubt about placing a shot during a rally, aim between your opponents, thus possibly creating confusion about which one of them should play the ball. A successful doubles team places far more emphasis on teamwork and tactics than on the sheer physical strength associated with singles.

**A QUICK INTERCEPT**
*A ball aimed diagonally between your opponents is always wise, but an alert net player may intercept it with a volley.*

# 98 DOUBLES TACTICS

The court area per player in doubles is smaller than in singles. Because the aim of all four players is to get to the net, it is essential to get at least 75 percent of your first serves into court. Sacrifice speed but maintain depth and accuracy.
- When receiving, keep your returns low over the net, unless you are lobbing, and aim 80 percent of them crosscourt, away from the server's partner at the net.
- If following in behind your service or return is difficult, play a groundstroke before advancing.
- The server's partner should cover toward the middle to help the server's net approach.

# 99 SERVING FORMATION

When playing doubles, one person plays in the right court, the other in the left. Each player is responsible for the shots in his half. If you cross to your partner's half, then he or she should move to your court to cover shots to that area.

*Server*

*Server's partner*

*Receiver's partner*

*Receiver*

**LEFT-HAND COURT SERVICE**

*Take up attack position in other half of court 9 ft (2.7 m) from net and halfway between center line and nearest doubles sideline; from here you can play aggressive volleys and smashes*

*Stand halfway between center mark and nearest doubles sideline. This will give you the best opportunity to cover all returns to your side of court*

**SERVER'S PARTNER**

**SERVER**

# 100 RECEIVING FORMATION

When receiving, start from the baseline area with your partner in midcourt. After deciding who receives in which court, keep these positions for the set. The receiver's partner should be able to advance to the net or retreat behind the baseline, as well as counter-volley if the server's partner intercepts your partner's return.

RECEIVER

RECEIVER'S PARTNER

*Stand inside service line, halfway between center line and doubles sideline*

*To return first services, stand behind baseline diagonally opposite server*

Server

Server's partner

Receiver's partner

Receiver

RIGHT-HAND COURT SERVICE

# 101 CHOOSING A PARTNER

Try playing with different partners until you find a player whose game complements your own. Being friends off the court can help you establish on-court rapport.

- If you prefer playing in the right court, find a partner who likes playing in the left, and vice versa.
- Make sure you both have the same ideas about tactics.

69

# INDEX

# ACKNOWLEDGMENTS

**Paul Douglas & Dorling Kindersley** would like to thank Hilary Bird for compiling the index; Ann Kay for proofreading; Mark Bracey for computer assistance; Alan Douglas, Craig Douglas, Ross McCue, and Melissa Traub for modeling; Pro Kennex (UK) Ltd of Wooburn Green, Bucks, First Service of Cobham, Surrey, and Sport & Ski of Woking Surrey, for supplying equipment; and the Hampshire Tennis & Health Club, West End, Southampton, and the Chris Lane Tennis & Health Club, Surrey, for location photography.

### Photography
All photography by Tim Ridley, Nick Goodall, and Matthew Ward, except for Colorsport, p. 65, and Robert Harding Picture Library, p. 67.

### Illustration
Craig Austin, Paul Dewhurst, Janos Marrfy,
Pete Sargent, and Rob Shone.

PUBLISHER'S NOTE
The instructions in this book are assumed for right-handed players,
and where appropriate should be reversed for left-handed players.